DATE DUE			
		·	

Maria
Montessori

Maria Montessori

Teacher of teachers

Marie Tennent Shephard

Lerner Publications Company • Minneapolis

Library of Congress Cataloging-in-Publication Data

Shephard, Marie Tennent.
  Maria Montessori : teacher of teachers / Marie Tennent Shephard.
      p. cm.
    Includes bibliographical references (p.   ) and index.
    Summary: Tells the story of the life of Italy's first female
physician and the creator of the Montessori method of education.
    ISBN 0-8225-4952-2 (alk. paper)
    1. Montessori, Maria, (1870–1952—Juvenile literature.
    2. Educators—Italy—Biography—Juvenile literature.
3. Montessori method of education—Juvenile literature.
[1. Montessori, Maria, 1870–1952. 2. Educators. 3.
Women–Biography. 4. Montessori method of education.] I. Title.
LB775.M8.S54 1996
370'.92—dc20   96-350

Manufactured in the United States of America
1 2 3 4 5 6 – JR – 01 00 99 98 97 96

Contents

Even as a young girl, Maria Montessori knew what she wanted.

ONE

From Ancona to Rome

1870–1881

"I'll be anything but a teacher." Twelve-year-old Maria's dark eyes flashed with determination. She had just completed elementary school and now her parents were discussing their plans for her future. As they talked in their comfortable, upper-middle-class apartment in Rome, Maria's declaration stunned her mother and father. With her usual self-assurance, Maria informed her parents that she wanted to attend a technical school to become an engineer.

An engineer! Totally unacceptable. In Italy in 1882, young women did not become engineers. Alessandro Montessori threw up his hands in horror. He could not acknowledge such an absurd request. After all, he was a respected official of the conservative Italian government. No child of his would defy tradition. He expected his only child to become a wife and mother. If she must have a career, she would be a teacher. He reminded Maria that if women worked outside the home, that was what they did.

Maria pictured the teachers she knew in her mind. They did not seem at all happy with their work. Instead they complained constantly of being underpaid and overworked.

She thought of the bored students, too. When Maria went to school, children sat on hard benches in drab, ugly schoolrooms. Books and teaching materials were scarce. Pupils listened to lectures, memorized facts, and then repeated their lessons like parrots. No wonder they had no desire to learn or think for themselves!

As Maria described the dismal life she would lead as a teacher, Renilde Montessori watched her pretty, talented daughter with secret pride. Was there a way she could convince Alessandro that Maria was right to want more out of her life?

Maria Montessori was born on August 31, 1870, in a four-story house in Chiaravalle in the seaport province of Ancona, Italy. Alessandro and Renilde often walked along the town wharf with Maria toddling beside them. She played at trying to catch the greedy seagulls that cruised about. The salty sea air smelled of fish whenever the family passed a boat's fresh catch. Ships bound for far-off ports took on boxes of goat cheese, grapes, or olives from the local farms.

Her father told stories of ancient times, of a colony of Greeks who fled from the Italian island of Sicily and finally settled in Ancona. Sometimes the family took a steamer ride across the Adriatic Sea to Zara or farther north to Fiume. Maria would point back to Ancona, a jut of land that curved into the sea. She felt very wise as she told those around her that Ancona meant "bend" in Greek.

Heads turned when the family went out walking together. Handsome, dignified Alessandro Montessori had dark curly hair and a full mustache. He wore a gold watch chain across his waistcoat. People passing would see Maria's

Maria's parents, Alessandro and Renilde, met in 1866.

mother, Renilde, and remark, "She's a beauty, that one!" She usually wore simple, stylish black dresses, perhaps with a little lace collar. Her only jewelry was a small gold cross. She would pile her hair on top of her head and set a rose in the black curls. The Montessoris proudly accepted compliments on their only child—a beautiful little girl with expressive jet-black eyes—as she danced along beside them.

Alessandro, a descendant of a noble family from Bologna, had been born in 1832. At age 16, he had received a medal for his part in a series of wars to free Italy from Austrian rule. In 1861 the wars resulted in the unification of Italy, a country formerly made up of kingdoms and principalities. Alessandro then worked as a financial clerk for the Italian government. By 1863 he had worked his way up to accountant for the ministry of finance in its salt and tobacco department, and was transferred to Chiaravalle in 1865. There he met and married Renilde Stoppani in 1866.

Renilde also came from a prosperous upper-class family. Very well educated, she loved books. She shared Alessandro's patriotic ideals for a unified Italy.

In 1870 Maria was born in Chiaravalle in the house on the right.

Renilde and Alessandro were strict parents. They believed small children needed discipline. One day when Maria was very young, she decided she was hungry. "I want something to eat," she said to her mother, who was busy unpacking from a family vacation. Renilde told Maria she would have to wait until mealtime. Finally, Maria's cries got so loud that her mother went to a cupboard. After the vacation, the cupboard was empty except for a moldy crust of bread. Renilde said quietly but firmly, "If you cannot wait, take this." Maria knew that she would get no fresh cheese or fruit until Mama was ready.

As a very small child, Maria once stopped a quarrel between her parents. She pushed a chair between them, climbed onto it, and clasped their hands together in hers.

She liked to wash squares of tile floor and count them as she washed. She might have been five years old when her mother taught her to knit so that she could make clothing for Italy's poor.

When Maria was five, the family moved to Rome. The Italian government had promoted her father, now an official in the state-run tobacco industry, to accountant first class. Alessandro had trouble adjusting to the active, growing city of Rome, which was far more modern than Chiaravalle. If his work had not forced him to move, he would have been content to stay in the quiet, slower-paced town. He did not welcome the change.

In Rome, elements of an ancient world existed in a 19th-century setting. The ruins of the Roman Empire towered over the busy city. Scholars, journalists, and artists carried on lively conversations and read newspapers at sidewalk cafés.

Unlike Alessandro, Renilde recognized the advantages

Rome was already a bustling city when the Montessoris moved there in 1875.

for Maria in Rome, a city rich in ancient history and art treasures in which one could learn. Rome offered galleries, museums, and libraries. The University of Rome was known as one of the finest universities in Europe. Together Renilde and

Maria explored the museums, the Colosseum, the Sistine Chapel, and other historic sights.

Although Maria could attend a more modern school in Rome than in Chiaravalle, elementary schools were crowded and poorly managed everywhere in Italy. The underpaid teachers themselves had little education. When Maria entered elementary school at age six, she thought of learning as something she had to do, like knitting for the poor. Maria did not strive to be the best pupil or the smartest. She could not understand why a classmate cried when a teacher did not promote her to the next grade. To Maria, one schoolroom was just like another.

In first grade, she won an award for good behavior. In second grade, she won an award for needlework, but this was not her favorite subject. Seven-year-old Maria found arithmetic and science more fun. The days when her teacher let the students leave the classroom and look for leaves, rocks, or animal tracks were Maria's favorites.

"Please remind me that I've made up my mind never to speak to you again," Maria Montessori said to a playmate when she was nine or ten years old. Although she was bossy, even snippy, with older children, she treated the younger ones kindly. Her playmates liked her to be their leader. She had them collect stones, sticks, and nuts and then made up games for them to play.

Maria sensed she had something important to do to help people in her future. When she was 10, she became so ill that her worried mother stayed at her bedside. Maria said, "Don't worry, Mama, I cannot die; I have too much to do."

When she was a student at the technical school, 16-year-old Maria posed for this photograph.

···◄ TWO ►···

Butterflies on Pins

1882–1892

Strong-minded Maria would not give up her goal. She would study to become an engineer even though her father refused to consider the idea. To prepare for an engineering career, 12-year-old Maria would have to attend a technical school in Rome.

Alessandro insisted that technical school was for boys. If girls continued their education after elementary school, they usually went to classical school. There the children spent hours learning Latin, Greek, and literature, and girls learned to cook and sew. Children attended classical school for five years. If they wished to continue, they enrolled for three more years to study classical literature. The course of study at a technical school lasted three years, followed by a four-year course at a technical institute.

Maria persisted. She wanted to study mathematics and science. Her father worked as an accountant. Why shouldn't she excel in math? In elementary school, Maria enjoyed solving arithmetic problems and earned high grades. She once took a textbook to the theater and studied in the dim light during the performance.

Renilde, more broad-minded than her husband, approved of her daughter's ambitions and encouraged her. Renilde had grown up in an era when upper-class teenage girls often lived in a convent until their parents chose husbands for them. By the time Maria was a teenager, people considered a mother's training at home best for a girl. Even married women did not have freedom. They could not travel alone or conduct business. All of their money belonged to their husbands.

Renilde supported Maria's desire to break away from the older ways. With her own adventurous spirit, Renilde may have wished she had been so bold as to try something no woman had done before. She finally persuaded her husband to allow their headstrong, talented girl to follow her dream. Both mother and daughter had the same stubborn streak. Alessandro was no match for them.

Maria's father had to inquire at several technical schools to find one that would enroll Maria. The principals feared that a spirited, pretty girl in class would distract the boys and the teachers. Alessandro assured one principal that Maria would sit in the back of the room and keep to herself.

Shortly after her 13th birthday in 1883, Maria enrolled in Regia Scuola Tecnica Michelangelo Buonarroti. The teachers forbade the only two female students to talk to the boys. At recess the girls went to a room with a guard at the door. Maria was lonely at school, but she knew Papa had gone out of his way to find a school to accept her. She told herself that studying math and science was more important than playing with the boys.

A school day consisted of classes for three hours in the morning, lunch at home, and classes for two hours in the afternoon. Maria had to sit passively for most of the five hours,

Most young girls Maria's age did not attend school with boys.
These Italian boys are on their way to school in Rome—with no
female classmates.

listening and repeating, listening and repeating. The students
studied plants by looking at a leaf in a book. They had no real
leaves to study and hold. Years later, Maria wrote, "The children, like butterflies mounted on pins, are fastened each to
his place, the desk, spreading the useless wings of barren
and meaningless knowledge which they have acquired."

In 1886 Maria graduated from technical school with a final
grade of 137 out of a possible 150 on her final examinations.

For the next four years, Maria attended Rome's technical institute, Regio Istituto Tecnico Leonardo da Vinci, and still intended to become an engineer. By the time she finished her studies at the institute, biology had caught her interest, and she began to think about studying medicine.

While walking in Rome's Pincio Park, Maria passed a shabby woman begging for alms. The woman's child sat on the cold ground and played with a piece of red paper. The little child, so absorbed and happy with such a simple thing as a scrap of paper, impressed Maria. This scene might have caused her sudden decision to become a doctor. Describing this incident to a friend, Maria said, "I cannot explain it. It just happened like that. You will probably think this is a very silly story: and if you told it to others they would probably just laugh at it."

An engineering career had been more than Alessandro could accept. Now Maria's plans to study medicine shocked him beyond belief. He refused to talk to her. Her friends and relatives—everyone except her mother—disapproved mightily. None of this daunted Maria. She snapped her fingers at all of them and made an appointment to see Dr. Guido Baccelli, head of the medical faculty at the University of Rome.

The professor listened politely to her request. It was out of the question, he said. A medical school would never admit a woman. As the interview ended, Maria shook his hand, thanked him, and said with confidence, "I *know* I shall become a doctor of medicine."

She enrolled in the University of Rome to take premedical classes in math, botany, physics, chemistry, and zoology. For the next two years, all that mattered were her studies. She had no time to attend parties, read romances, or sit with friends in cafés.

In 1892, with a grade of 8 out of a possible 10, she received the university's *Diploma di Licenza.* If she had been a man, she could have enrolled in medical school automatically. As a woman, she could not expect admittance to the male-dominated world of medicine. Still, Maria persisted, with her mother's strong support.

She tried every way she could think of to get into medical school. She wrote letters, she sent character references from former teachers, and she asked friends to speak for her. Years later, Maria said she even appealed to Pope Leo XIII, who told her that medicine was a worthy profession for women.

Though no one knows exactly how, the door to a career in medicine finally opened for Maria Montessori. In 1892 she became the first female student of medicine at the University of Rome.

As a medical student and a lecturer, Maria was known for her beauty and her intelligence.

◄ THREE ►

Into the Lion's Den

1892–1896

The university accepted Maria as a medical student, but the male students did not. They showed their resentment in every way they could. They made sure she heard their unflattering remarks. She waited outside the lecture hall until the men had taken their seats so she would not come in contact with them. In the small hall where professors lectured and conducted chemistry experiments, her fellow students deliberately left no seat for her.

She responded to the men's jokes good-naturedly. When the students whistled at her in the halls, she sang a little rhyme to them with a smile, "Blow away, my friends. The harder you blow, the higher up I shall go." A fellow who sat behind her waggled his foot to make her desk shake. Maria turned and glared at him. She laughed as she heard him whisper to another student, "Did you see the look she gave me? I must be immortal—I should be dead!"

"In those days," Maria said, "I felt as if I could have done anything."

Not only did the men resent a woman in their midst, but they resented that this woman was a better student than many of them. Her serious interest in learning pleased the instructors. She attended all lectures, although the university did not require full attendance. Her classmates attended classes when they felt like it. If they missed a lecture, they would borrow someone else's notes. University students spent most of their time frequenting cafés and wandering about town. Many students only attended medical school so they could call themselves doctors. Most did not intend to practice medicine. But Maria planned to be a practicing doctor.

The system of education at this higher level was not much more challenging to the bright Maria than her earlier schooling had been. Universities required students only to read, memorize, and repeat the answers on oral and written exams at the end of the year.

One night a fierce snowstorm battered Rome. This was not a night for anyone to be outdoors. The students used the storm as a good excuse to stay away from class—but not Maria. Shivering, and with the hem of her long skirt wet from the deep snow, she arrived at the classroom to find only the professor. Thoughtful Maria felt guilty that the professor should have to lecture to one student. In spite of her protests, he insisted on giving his lecture to such a devoted student. Maria remembered it as the most peaceful of lectures.

Although Maria was now 22, her father often walked her to class. A proper young woman did not walk the streets alone. Alessandro walked in silence and showed no interest in her studies or her problems. He could not adjust to Maria's independence. Not only had his daughter chosen a career unfit for a woman, but she had financed it herself by winning scholarships and tutoring other students. Maria longed for her father's approval. He had stopped being the warm-hearted, sympathetic Papa she had always known.

At least she had her mother's support and encouragement. Renilde took great interest and pleasure in helping her daughter. She listened as Maria read from her notes, and the two women discussed Maria's lessons. Renilde separated Maria's heavy textbooks into sections to make them easier to carry and then had them bound back together at the end of the year.

Outwardly, Maria kept up her cheerful attitude, but having no one at the university with whom she could talk or laugh or share ideas was hard for her. She suffered her worst disappointment when her professors told her she must not attend dissecting classes with the other students. Men and women could not view a naked body, even a dead one, together. So Maria had to work with the corpses in the evenings—alone.

For the first lesson at the Institute of Anatomy, Maria arrived before the professor. In a letter to a friend, she later described how nervous she had been as she wandered around the long, dark room. The only light came from one open window.

Her only company was a human skeleton hanging in the corner. The skeleton seemed larger to her than any human. She stared at it for a long time, then moved on to a cupboard with jars of internal organs floating in liquid. At the other end of the room, almost in darkness, sat a row of skulls on a shelf. Written on the foreheads in black ink were the words "murderer" and "thief." Next to each skull was a brain.

Maria felt cold and began to shake. The whole scene sickened her. She said to herself, "My God, what have I done to suffer this way? Why me all alone in the midst of all this death?" She went back to stand in front of the skeleton. It seemed to move. "Come, come! These are only feelings," she thought. "The skeleton does not budge. And what is a skeleton after all?"

Outside the window, she could see lights, people, and colors in the street. Everything out there looked beautiful to her. The sight of a young woman standing in the doorway of a hat shop made her feel jealous. That woman was free and everyone around her was alive. The woman had only her hats and a good sale on her mind.

But Maria did not run from the skeleton, the skulls, or the organs. She leaned against the wall. Her knees were weak and her heart pounded. She kept her eyes glued to the gleam of light from the window. She loved all things outside that room.

When the professor arrived, an attendant brought a basin into the room. The basin contained bones with pink flesh clinging to them and something dark, soft, and horrible smelling. Maria shuddered as she remembered they were once parts of a person who had suffered. She touched the human organs. They felt rubbery and slimy. She struggled to calm herself and listen to the professor, but she couldn't. The blood pulsing through her head almost overpowered her. Somehow she managed to keep from fainting.

When she returned home, her family could tell she was upset. Her father said, "It is useless for you to force yourself, you can't."

Her mother agreed, saying, "It is bad for you, my child, don't go back."

"It is the first time," Maria replied. "At least I did not faint." She left them, went to her room, and threw up.

In her bed that night, she remembered how the skeleton had horrified her. How would a corpse affect her? She had never seen death. Through the night she slept fitfully. Why

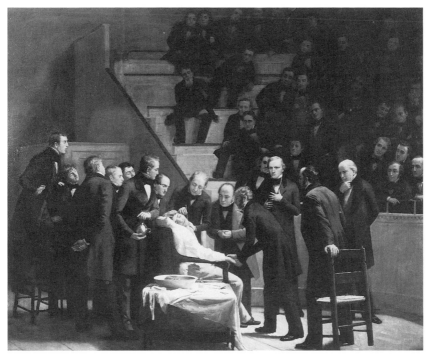

This painting shows the demonstration of surgical anesthesia in the late 1880s. Only men were allowed in the class. Women were not allowed to view a naked body with their male classmates.

had she ever decided to study anatomy? But what of the future, the goal of becoming a doctor? What a splendid goal! No, the road leading there was too awful, she argued with herself. She wouldn't be able to do anyone any good. Better to be a dressmaker, a servant. . . . Oh, but not that, not *that!*

Finally, in her exhausted and fitful state, Maria made up her mind. She would write to the professor, thank him for the first day's lesson, and apologize for not continuing. To study human anatomy seemed impossible. With her mind eased by this solution, she fell into a short sleep. By morning she felt better.

She looked for arguments to support her decision to quit. No one would want a woman doctor. Even other women preferred that men treat them. She thought of her isolation, the hostility of her classmates, and the awful, sickening stench in the anatomy room. Worst of all, her father's coldness toward her disturbed her. She had very valid reasons to abandon her dream.

But Maria never wrote the letter to her professor. She had chosen medicine. This was her mission. She must learn to handle organs and cut through flesh. She willed herself to ignore the sights and smells. Plucky Maria disciplined herself to keep her feelings under control and she became an excellent surgeon.

Like the little girl who knitted for the poor and went to school, she would do what she had to do. Maria often said, "We are not born simply to enjoy ourselves."

In her second year at medical school, the men acted friendlier. They could not help admiring their spunky classmate who laughed at their scoffing remarks. Some of them would probably have liked to court this lovely, attractively dressed young woman. What young man would not want people to see him out walking with the fascinating Maria on his arm? But she was too busy studying to be a doctor to accept invitations.

She did participate when a group of students organized a festival of flowers in the spring of 1892. Costumed owners of the most beautifully decorated carriages received prizes. That year first prize went to Queen Margherita of Italy. The students chose Maria to present the award. The queen asked that the prize be given to another contestant. Maria, in her quiet and tactful way, insisted the queen accept it. Her Highness could not refuse the gracious young student.

People singled out Maria Montessori, not only as the first female medical student, but as the recipient of awards and assignments. She won a scholarship of a thousand *lire,* which was a great deal of money in the 1890s. When asked how the men reacted when a woman won this prize, she admitted that they were a bit grumpy.

Maria competed for and won a position as assistant in the hospital run by the university. She could now gain valuable experience in the care of patients a year before her graduation. The medical school directors also permitted her to work at the children's hospital and to assist at surgery in the accident ward there. Treating children sparked her interest and started her career as a child specialist.

Before graduation, each student had to give a lecture to the other students and the faculty. The university invited the public to these events. On the day of Maria's lecture, her father's friend suggested to him that they attend together. "What lecture?" asked Alessandro, since he had no knowledge of Maria's activities. Embarrassed at seeming to be an uninterested parent, he attended with his friend.

In her lecture, Maria talked of how much the medical profession meant to her and delighted the audience with her touches of humor. She had expected that her fellow students would boo and hiss at her. Instead she received an ovation. She said afterward, "I felt like a lion tamer that day."

The applause and shouts had come as a surprise, but her father's reaction pleased her most of all. After being congratulated as the father of a warm, charming daughter who spoke so brilliantly, he could refer proudly to his daughter, the doctor.

Maria's Doctor of Medicine diploma from the University of Rome

Maria wrote a paper as the final requirement for graduation. Her 96 handwritten pages discussed paranoia, a mental illness. She appeared before 11 examiners to discuss her research. Beautifully dressed and wearing gloves and a hat, she impressed the examiners with her musical voice, her grace, and her mind—as sharp as any of the male students'.

Maria waited outside the room while the examiners totaled her score. Each could allow up to 10 points. Anything over 100 was an exceptional score. Maria received a final grade of 105.

When the committee called her back into the room, they awarded Maria Montessori, at age 25, the degree of Doctor of Medicine. On July 10, 1896, she became the first female doctor in Italy.

"So, here I am: famous!" Maria wrote to a friend. She had heard people say they couldn't believe that a young woman who looked "delicate and rather shy" could stand the sight and smell of corpses. How could the one woman in a group of men look and touch naked bodies? "I am not famous because of my skill or intelligence," she wrote, "but for my courage and indifference toward everything. This is something which, if one wishes, one can always achieve, but it takes tremendous efforts."

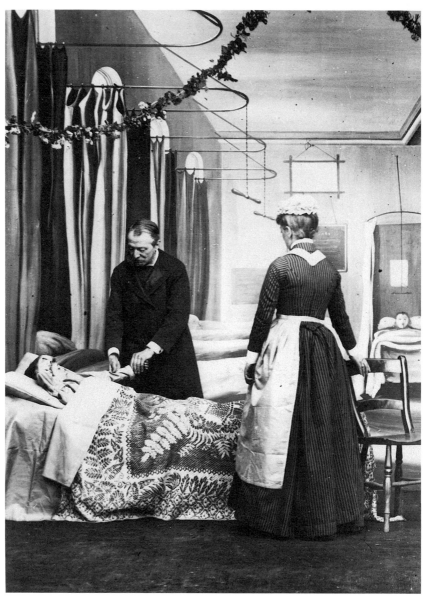

Like the patient pictured here, most children in hospitals of the late 1800s were cared for by male doctors. The University of Rome, however, hired Maria as a children's doctor.

···◀ FOUR ▶···

Like a Shining Light
1896–1901

With her student days over, Dr. Montessori took on a schedule that kept her busy from morning to night. As a single woman, she still lived with her parents in their Rome apartment, but she was now a professional and brought home an income. The staff at the university children's hospital knew of her skill as a surgeon and her compassion as a physician. They sent patients to her, and she began to build a private practice.

Asked how patients felt about having a female doctor and one so young, the *dottoressa*—as Italians called her—said that people wanted her services. They knew when someone really cared about them.

The dottoressa was more than a doctor to her patients. She was a nurse, a cook, and a servant as well. She once stayed with a small boy who was seriously ill with pneumonia. She gave him a warm bath, made his bed, and fixed him nourishing soup. The mother wrote a letter of thanks, saying that the dottoressa had saved her child's life. Renilde Montessori kept the letter with many others that her daughter received from grateful patients.

31

A mother had given birth to twins who became seriously ill. The mother feared that her children were close to death and begged her husband to send for the dottoressa. At first he refused. They could not afford a doctor, but he had to try to save his babies and finally agreed. When Dr. Montessori arrived, she took charge immediately. She sent the mother to bed, lit the fire, and heated water to bathe the infants. Maria fed them, held them lovingly, and stayed with them, hour after hour, until she knew the infants were out of danger.

Maria's reputation grew. In 1896 a group of learned and powerful women from around the world gathered in Berlin to discuss the poor living conditions of women and to call for better opportunities for women everywhere. The Italian women who attended this international women's congress asked Maria to represent them as a delegate. Maria was delighted to accept the honor. She knew that much had to be done to improve the wretched working conditions of women. She believed that women could and should do more with their lives. They should seek careers along with being wives and mothers.

Maria had the delegates' full attention as she eloquently presented her practical ideas. She told them that she was speaking on behalf of six million Italian women—the women who worked 18 hours a day in factories and on farms. Their pay was half of what men earned for the same work, and some women earned even less than that. Daily pay for women in the candle factories was equal to 20 cents in the United States, and those working in the mills received only 12 cents. The delegates unanimously adopted Maria's proposal that women get equal pay for equal work.

Maria never used notes for her speeches. When a reporter asked to see a copy of her lecture, she smiled and showed him papers she had been holding as a prop. They were blank.

The young, beautiful doctor became a celebrity at the convention. Reporters described her as "standing out like a beacon, a shining light among the other women." They wrote of her beautiful voice, warm smile, and dainty gestures—her hands as graceful as a ballet dancer's. One description read, "The distinguished lady in the photograph is lovely looking—dark eyes, a Mona Lisa smile, a frilled collar, and a strand of pearls setting off the face framed with soft curls."

On the way back to Rome, she wrote to her parents that many newspapers had mentioned her. But a person so dedicated to her work preferred to read of her achievements and not her beauty. She said, "My face will not appear in the papers any more and no one shall dare to sing my so-called charms again. I shall do serious work."

As an assistant doctor at the university's psychiatric clinic, Dr. Montessori visited the city's hospitals for mentally ill and disabled patients to determine if the university clinic might help some of them. Although she had studied mental illnesses, for the first time she could observe mentally disabled children.

At one of the hospitals, she found a group of children crawling about the floor and grabbing crumbs to eat or play with. As Dr. Montessori watched the children with dismay, the caretaker said, "They're disgusting. Dirty and greedy, too!"

"In what way?" the dottoressa asked.

The caretaker shrugged. "When they have finished a meal, they throw themselves on the floor and act like animals. They pick up crumbs, play with them, then put them in their mouths!"

Looking about the bare room, Dr. Montessori saw that

Disabled and homeless children in Rome's hospitals had few, if any, toys and no chance for an education.

the children had nothing to stimulate their minds, nothing to look at, nothing to touch except those crumbs. Maria thought these children needed balls to throw, dolls to cuddle, and toys to develop their hand muscles.

Maria searched the libraries for any information she could find on mentally disabled children. She studied the works of two French doctors, Jean-Marc-Gaspard Itard and his student Edouard Séguin. These scientists had devoted their lives to the education of mentally disabled children.

Itard and Séguin believed these children needed special education rather than special medical treatment. Dr. Montessori agreed. She believed that children without proper care and education could become delinquents.

In 1897, Maria lectured at a national medical congress in Turin, Italy, and a year later at a national teacher's congress there. Each time she spoke, she promoted the education of disabled children. She maintained that those locked away in hospitals deserved to learn to do simple work.

Maria referred her audiences to the work of Séguin. He had written that a mentally disabled child could learn, but only if the method of teaching was adapted to the child's particular abilities. Institutions in western Europe, England, and the United States had carried out his ideas. Maria said that these institutions had helped thousands of mentally disabled people to work and support themselves. Italy did not have any institutions of this kind. These people had received training in gardening, tailoring, shoemaking, masonry, and many other trades. Teachers could train the more severely disabled children to make candles, brooms, or cane chairs, she said. Maria warned her audience to work toward understanding these children who do not adjust well to society and to help them stay out of trouble.

Maria's articles began appearing in various publications throughout Italy. In 1898, she wrote an article for the magazine *Roma* entitled "Social Miseries and New Scientific Discoveries." So many people wanted to read this article that the issue sold out.

Dr. Montessori was a popular subject for the press. Newspapers reported on her speeches. When people read about Maria, they flocked to hear the "beautiful scholar" speak. She traveled throughout Europe lecturing on her ideas for the special education of mentally disabled children and on "The New Woman."

She told her audience that the new woman was not yet trained to compete with men in the world. A woman needed to demonstrate her strength and her ability to work just as well as men. The new woman is a pioneer who must learn to speak for her own rights. The crowds applauded Maria wildly and shouted, *"Brava! Brava!"*

Besides the speeches, her private practice, and her work at several hospitals, Dr. Montessori served as a professor at the University of Rome and as an examiner there, reading students' research papers. At a women's teacher-training college called the Regio Istituto Superiore di Magistero Femminile, she gave lectures in hygiene and anthropology, the study of humanity. Enthusiastic students told other students about Dr. Montessori's lively lectures, and soon her lecture halls filled with inspired students.

Anna Maria Maccheroni was one of these students. She described the first time she heard Dr. Montessori lecture. "She spoke—not about anthropology, but about schools. She told us what a school should be like . . . . She was a most attractive lecturer: her language was so simple, so clear, her delivery so animated, that even the poorer students could understand her."

Dr. Guido Baccelli, the official who had refused to admit Maria to medical school, was now Italy's minister of public education. Maria's speeches so impressed him that he asked her to lecture to Rome's teachers on how to educate children with learning disabilities.

The study of education became all-important to Maria. As she read educational theories that had been written during the previous 200 years, she discovered important ideas

Dr. Guido Baccelli was impressed by Maria's ideas for educating children with learning disabilities.

that she wanted to develop into a new way of teaching disabled children.

In 1898 Rome officials planned to open a state school to train teachers in the education of "these unhappy little ones," as Maria called mentally disabled children. As part of their training, the teachers ran a practice school, which enrolled 22 pupils when it opened. The state officials appointed Dr. Montessori as a director of this Orthophrenic School. ("Ortho" means correction of deformities and "phrenic" refers to the mind.)

Maria and her co-director at the school, Dr. Giuseppe Montesano, worked closely together to develop a program that would help these children. Soon Maria and Giuseppe fell in love. Sometime between 1898 and 1900, Maria gave birth to a child that she named Mario. She and Giuseppe never married, possibly because their families did not approve. Giuseppe promised Maria that he would never marry anyone else.

For an unmarried woman to have a child was scandalous. Maria would have ruined her career and embarrassed her mother and father if she had let the world know that Mario was her son. To avoid scandal, she sent the baby to live with a family in the country and visited him whenever she could.

For her 30th birthday in 1900, Maria received a wonderful surprise. Her proud father had clipped out all of the articles about his daughter from the Italian, French, German, and English newspapers for the previous eight years. He had pasted over 200 items into an elegant leather album. In his beautiful handwriting, he included a table of contents and listed dates, cities, and publications. This outpouring of her father's love and pride in her accomplishments probably made this one of Maria's happiest birthdays.

When the Orthophrenic School opened in 1900, Maria continued her work with Dr. Montesano. She devoted her days to teaching the children and to observing and advising the other teachers at the school. She worked from eight in the morning until seven in the evening. Each night she spent hours making notes on the pupils' reactions to her methods and improvements she could make to her teaching materials.

Many hours of study and experimentation paid off. Success with these pupils removed all doubt that she could teach her "unhappy little ones" to read and write. Maria began by teaching the simplest motions—using a spoon, walking on a straight line. She then trained the senses, first with walks in the garden to see and smell flowers, then with various textured objects to feel and develop the sense of touch. She taught the alphabet by having the children touch raised letters.

She later recalled that some of the mentally disabled students learned to read and write fairly well. "I was able to present them at a public school for an examination together with normal children. And they passed the examination successfully." She had worked with these children for only two years.

Educators called Dr. Montessori a miracle worker. The little girl who said, "I'll be anything but a teacher," had become one.

At her Children's House, Maria directs a child in the use of her special teaching materials.

◄ FIVE ►

An Unknown Mission

1901–1907

Now Maria gave herself a new challenge. If mentally disabled children could learn so well and so quickly, why shouldn't healthy, bright children do much better work in school than they did?

Again she listened to her intuition. She sensed that if she applied the same teaching methods used at the Orthophrenic School to normal children, she could "develop or set free their personality in a marvelous and surprising way."

"It was almost as if I prepared myself for an unknown mission," Maria said.

She enrolled again at the University of Rome, this time as a student of philosophy and psychology to better understand normal children and their learning problems. She turned her duties at the Orthophrenic School over to the capable teachers she had trained and cut back still more on her hospital work and private practice.

Maria may have had a more personal reason to leave the school that she had worked so hard to create. Dr. Montesano had broken his promise never to marry. In 1901 when he did marry someone else, Maria left the school.

She returned to Edouard Séguin's study of disabled children. She hunted all over Rome for his second book. Finally a friend found a filthy, musty copy in New York. When the book arrived, Alessandro disinfected it before he would let his daughter use it. Maria translated and copied Séguin's two books from French into Italian by hand. She also copied books by Dr. Jean-Marc-Gaspard Itard. By using this study method, she remembered what she had read and had time to ponder the authors' words.

Maria sat in elementary schoolrooms in Rome and watched children, "like butterflies mounted on pins," as they listened, memorized, and repeated their lessons. The sight brought back memories of her own boring school days.

At last, the opportunity she had hoped for came—to apply the methods used with disabled children to normal preschoolers. In a slum of Rome called San Lorenzo, people lived in tumbledown tenement houses and crowded, unsanitary conditions. Crime ruled the streets. The Roman Association of Good Building decided to clean up the area and rebuild the houses. The association added trees and landscaping to a courtyard. They rented apartments to married couples in the hope that the tenants would take pride in their new homes and keep them in good repair. But the tenants' children who were two to six years old were too young to attend school. Left alone all day while their parents worked, the youngsters marked up clean walls, threw things into the fountain, and trampled plants.

Edoardo Talamo, director general of the association, suggested that they set aside a room for the children with a caretaker to watch them during the day. Paying a children's caretaker would cost less than constantly repairing the building. Members of the association asked Dr. Montessori if she would accept the position. They asked her to take complete charge of 50 children.

The association offered nothing else, just the children and one cheerless room inside the tenement house. The association gave no thought to buying equipment. But Maria's dream had come true. She could train the children without interference from anyone. She would take these 50 extremely poor, timid, and neglected ragamuffins, place them in the best environment she could create, and see what they could do.

When Maria first walked through the dirty, desolate streets of San Lorenzo, she realized the area needed much work to eliminate poverty and vice. The people she passed had no joy in their pale faces. No carriages rolled by. The street vendors seen in other neighborhoods did not call out their wares here. No happy tunes came from an organ-grinder's hand organ. Maria sensed the despair of these people, who lived in a world of shadows and misery.

Friends of Maria's family could not understand her. How could Maria—a doctor, a university professor—give herself up to taking care of children in a slum? In her usual, determined way, Maria went ahead with her plans and ignored her friends' disapproval.

She had small chairs and tables made for the children that were light enough for them to move around by themselves. She expected criticism for allowing the children to knock the chairs and tables about and create noise and disorder. She insisted this would not happen at her school. If a chair fell over noisily, a child would learn to pick it up quietly. The children would acquire grace and agility in moving their tables and would be free to place them wherever they wished. The traditional schools with desks bolted to the floor did not allow for the "command of movement" that Maria felt children needed. She would place everything—shelves, cupboards, chalkboards, and washstands—at a child's height. For funds, she asked some wealthy friends who had helped other causes, and also used money of her own.

Someone suggested the name *Casa dei Bambini,* or Children's House, for the room. Maria liked the name, and that is what she called her school.

Casa dei Bambini opened on January 6, 1907, the Feast of the Epiphany. Epiphany is a Roman Catholic feast day with a Christmas tree and presents for children. Maria believed she too would give them a gift—a new education.

In a special ceremony for invited guests, Dr. Montessori planned to make a speech. The 50 children of the school dressed alike in stiff, oversized blue smocks.The adults had to drag the tearful, scared children to the ceremony. They

Maria made sure that all furniture, even the cupboards, were child-sized.

knew nothing of the world outside the dark tenement houses, and the sight of an audience of strangers terrified them. Someone had taught the children to make a military salute, but they were too frightened to move. They had to be led away without putting on their show. They were afraid of everything, even the Christmas tree and presents. One audience member remarked, "I wonder if there will ever be any change in these children."

As Dr. Montessori spoke that day, she had a vision. She announced that the work they undertook would prove to be very important. Someday people would come from all over the world to see the results.

These words amazed the audience. What could she expect the poor, shy little children to do that would interest anyone?

The Children's House, this school within a house, offered free child care to all the tenement's working parents with two- to six-year-old children. Maria posted rules that required parents to send their children "clean in body and clothing and provided with a suitable apron" and to cooperate with the teacher in the children's education. Maria's combination of family and school in one building created a new idea in education. At any time, parents were welcome to watch their children work and to become friends with the teacher. Like the wealthy, these parents could say that they had left their children in the care of a governess or nurse. The San Lorenzo parents also received a chart that showed their child's growth and condition.

Maria concerned herself with the whole child—not only how well a child developed mentally, but physically too. Still a doctor, Maria developed a system for recording each child's weight and measurements. Every month, she measured each child standing and sitting. She weighed them after their weekly baths. (She preferred to give daily baths, but she found daily baths for 50 children to be impossible.)

For the times she could not be in the schoolroom, Maria chose an assistant, Candida Nuccitelli, who lived in one of the tenement apartments. Candida knew the families and their problems and could gain their confidence. She had no training in standard teaching methods, so she could adapt to Maria's new ways. For instance, Maria believed that a teacher should not teach the children, but should direct them. In her schools, she used the title of "directress" for her female teachers. The directress showed the children how to use the materials, then let them work on their own. She must sit and watch, Maria said, "like the astronomer who sits immovable before the telescope while the worlds whirl through space." Maria wanted to hear a teacher say, "The children are now working as if I did not exist."

Maria gave Candida no special duties. She just showed her assistant how to present materials correctly to the children. "I told her not to interfere with the children in any way or I would not be able to observe them."

She brought in materials she had created to teach the Orthophrenic School students, but she expected the students at Casa dei Bambini to flock to the balls, dolls, and other toys that people had donated to the school. Instead, they preferred her learning materials, such as the pink tower, the knobbed cylinders, and the dressing frames.

Maria believed that children learn by using their five senses. She regarded little children's hands and sensitive fingertips as learning tools. She insisted that hands be spotlessly clean for feeling around a triangle or judging dimensions of knobbed cylinders because clean fingers

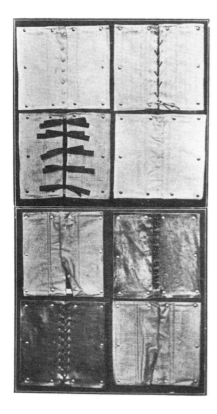

Maria used these frames for lacing and buttoning to teach children manual dexterity.

"touch better." These children of the slums soon learned to wash before using any of the materials. They discovered the fun of using the small pitchers and bowls at the little wash-stands. Before the children came to Maria's school, they had never thought about cleanliness. Now, they ran around showing everyone, "See! Clean hands!"

Maria made up bottles of different scents for smelling and flavors for tasting. She filled bottles with water from hot to cold. Boxes contained sand, seeds, or stones for hearing soft to loud sounds. The children enjoyed being blindfolded to learn to "see without eyes" when they matched scraps of fabric by feel.

Blindfolded children use the sense of touch to feel different textures.

Maria designed these materials to develop concentration and observation. She wanted to help her students learn to compare and to make decisions. These sense exercises provided the foundation for speech, writing, and mathematics.

Maria made so many things for little fingers to do. Children learned from the wooden dressing frames to fasten hooks and eyes and tie bows. The button frame had two pieces of cloth fastened to a wooden frame with buttons down one piece and buttonholes on the other. She watched the children button and unbutton, time after time. Lacing frames taught girls how to lace the bodices worn by Italian women.

Maria covered small wood squares with silk thread in eight shades of a color, such as purple, from light to dark. A child could place the eight tablets in a row so they looked like a strip of ribbon shaded pale lavender to deep purple.

The children liked to play "poker" with the color tablets. One child acted as dealer. A player asked for red tablets, another for green, another for orange, and so on. When each child collected all eight shades of one color, the group raced to see who could place the tablets in the correct light-to-dark order first.

Three-year-old Lucia would rather build the pink tower with the cubes of different sizes than cuddle a doll. Maria showed her how to pick up and stack the 10 blocks. She gave no help other than to demonstrate by building the tower slowly with as little movement as possible. Lucia had difficulty grasping the large cube in her tiny hand. Finally she managed by using both hands. Clapping and laughing, she added the other blocks. Maria left the little girl to work by herself. Lucia saw how the cubes fit one on top of the other and discovered that she could build a perfect pink tower by

Children as young as three years old learned about size differences by playing with the pink tower.

herself. Her fingertips "saw" the size of each cube before her eyes did. Proud Lucia built tower after tower.

Maria designed each apparatus so that a child using it in the right order in the right way could see a mistake and correct it without an adult's interference. Observing how Lucia had taught herself to build the pink tower made Maria happy. She could see Lucia was learning independence, self-control, and self-confidence just as Maria had hoped.

Maria's dressing frames with ribbons and buttons help teach children to dress themselves.

"Playing" with the knobbed cylinders

The children enjoyed repetition, Maria learned. As Sophia fit the knobbed cylinders into holes in four long wooden blocks, she put them in and took them out at least 40 times. Maria shook her head, amazed at Sophia's concentration as she sat so contentedly doing the exercise again and again.

Maria watched little children at work for hours and always listened carefully to whatever they had to say. To her, the child was the real teacher.

Before long, Maria's youngest students at the Casa dei Bambini had learned to write.

SIX

Explosions
1907–1908

Maria's personality drew people, young and old, to her. When Maria entered the room, the children ran to greet her. To her, every child was important. Her love reached out to each one. She came in smiling, elegantly and tastefully dressed, her dark hair a neat pile on top of her head.

Maria was now in her late 30s, plump but strikingly beautiful. She still lived with her parents in Rome and visited Mario in boarding school as often as she could.

As the weeks passed at the Casa dei Bambini, Maria saw remarkable changes in the children. Maria's charges, once dirty, withdrawn, and rebellious, had become well behaved, happy, outgoing, and eager to learn. The children reaped the rewards of her new ideas for education. She gave them the freedom to learn by doing things for themselves at their own speed. Each child could proudly say, "I learned. Nobody taught me."

Mothers appreciated what was happening at the school and in their own homes. Children told their parents, "Your hands are dirty," or "You should clean those stains off your clothes." The parents paid attention. Broken pots disappeared from windowsills and blossoming geraniums replaced them. Windows sparkled.

Even the youngest children could wash and dress themselves, clean the classroom, and keep it in perfect order. They began asking to read and write. Their mothers asked, too. Since their youngsters had learned so much so quickly, shouldn't the children be ready to read?

Although Maria had given no thought to teaching those under six to read, she recalled that the disabled children had learned. She had taught them with an alphabet of wooden letters that had vowels painted red and consonants blue.

Unable to find another wooden alphabet that she could afford, Maria made letters of paper and cardboard. At the end of the day, Anna Fedeli, one of Maria's students at the teacher-training college, helped her make the new letters. They sat at a little table, their long skirts sweeping the floor, and cut, painted, and glued. As they worked, Maria had an idea. Besides the cardboard letters, they would make alphabets of sandpaper. What better preparation for writing than tracing with the fingertips around rough letters? The next day she brought in a sack of sandpaper and set to work.

Soon little fingers moved busily over the homemade letters in the classroom. The children learned that each letter represented a sound. The room buzzed with the sounds of the alphabet. When they put the letters side by side on the mat, they could make words like *m-a-m-m-a*. Zaira announced, "To make *Zaira,* I must have *z-a-i-r-a*. I must have *z-a-i-r-a*."

On a sunny December day, Maria took the children up to the roof of the Casa dei Bambini. As she sat by a chimney, she handed a piece of chalk to Pietro and said, "Draw me a picture of this chimney."

He drew his picture. Then he wrote on the tile the word *mano* (hand). With a burst of joy, he cried out, "I can write! I can write!" Pietro wrote *camino* (chimney), *tetto* (roof), and *mamma*. "I can write! I know how to write!" he shouted again.

The other children gathered around waiting to try. They said, "Give me the chalk. I can write, too!" They wrote words, names, and more words. They were so excited that Maria said, "They might be compared to the hen who has just laid an egg."

This "explosion into writing," as Maria called it, spread among the children like a fire in the forest. She had ignited a spark, an eagerness to put down words wherever the children found a bare spot. They filled up the chalkboards. Some children stood on chairs to write on the board above their

Maria made these cardboard letters for the children at the first Casa dei Bambini in San Lorenzo.

classmates' heads. They pulled Maria around the room to admire words they had written in chalk on the floor. She said, "For days we walked on a carpet of written signs."

Mothers described children going to bed with pencil and paper in hand. Two of the four-year-olds sent neatly written thank-you notes and Christmas greetings to Edoardo Talamo, the person responsible for the Casa dei Bambini.

This all happened, Maria said, "while the children in the first elementary [grades] were laboriously working . . . to prepare for making the curves of 'o' and the other vowels."

Learning to read, Maria discovered, came after learning to write. Some weeks went by as the children put all their energy into writing with no thought of reading. One day Maria wrote on the board, "If you love me, give me a kiss" and "If you can read this, come to me."

For several days, nothing happened. "They thought," she said, "that I was writing for *my* own amusement, and they were writing for *their* own joy." On the fourth day, Mia came to her and said, "Here I am." Bella ran up to kiss her.

Another explosion—they tried reading everything with letters on it. Parents said that when they went for a walk, their children had to stop at every little shop, theater, or poster, any place with words to read.

Maria made up cards with the names of toys on them. She put the cards into a basket and a child drew out a card. If the child read the name of the toy correctly, he or she could play with the toy. But the children wanted to draw out cards and read them, not play with the toys.

Maria continued to marvel at her students' desire for work over play. She said, "I watched them, seeking to understand the secret of these souls, of whose greatness I had been so ignorant! As I stood in meditation among the eager children, the discovery that it was knowledge they loved, and not the silly *game,* filled me with wonder and made me think of the greatness of the human soul!"

A second Casa dei Bambini opened in April 1907 in another of the San Lorenzo tenement buildings. Word spread around Rome that "something wonderful and revolutionary" was happening in the slums of San Lorenzo. Those who ventured down the filthy, dismal streets of the tenement quarter to see for themselves came away with astonishing reports. Children not much older than babies had learned to write in two months' time and to read soon after. Observers remarked that if they had not seen this for themselves, they would never have believed it.

Visitors recalled entering a large cheerful room that had an air of quiet activity. Everything seemed to be at a low level, even the hum of voices. Here and there, Maria had scattered little tables and chairs painted in bright colors. She brought plants, a fishbowl, and pictures of flowers, animals, and religious scenes to make the room homey. The windows looked out onto a garden.

Fifty young pupils worked at tables or on small mats on the floor with strange-looking objects. Some children looked up and smiled. A few ran up to say good morning. Others were so absorbed that they didn't notice strangers in the room.

At first glance, no adult seemed to supervise. Off in a corner, a young woman sat on the floor with two tiny girls. She quietly watched as the girls ran their fingers around the edges of circles, squares, and triangles.

The children in Maria's classroom were often busy with "exercises of practical life," what Maria called household chores.

What an unusual sight! In this large group of children, no one ran, fought, or even talked loudly.

When Benito misbehaved, Maria went to him first and told him to sit by himself at a table in a corner. He could play with whatever he wanted, but she told the others that he was "not well." They must stay away from him until he was "well." Maria spoke to him soothingly, with no scolding, as she might talk to a baby. Then she talked to the others as if they were much more mature. She could not say why this form of discipline had an effect, but afterwards the isolated one always showed pride in his work and behavior, and a tender affection for Maria.

People asked Maria how there could be a schoolroom full of children with none of the usual discipline. She answered, "A room in which all the children move usefully, intelligently, and voluntarily without committing any rough or rude act would seem to me to be a classroom very well disciplined indeed."

As a day at Casa dei Bambini began, the children washed themselves, even behind their ears, and brushed their teeth at the low washstands. The five- and six-year-olds helped the younger ones.

Then they tidied up the Casa, their home for the day. Out came gaily colored feather dusters, small brooms, and dustpans painted green with red dots. The girls and boys turned to cleaning like finicky housekeepers. They watered the plants, fed the fish, and checked the shelves to see that everything was in place. Maria called these chores "exercises of practical life."

The housework done, the children might sing or talk with Maria or Candida. Then the children were free to choose whatever materials they wished.

All activity in the classroom stopped when a sign with the word *Silenzio* (Silence) appeared on the chalkboard. The children sat motionless at the tables. Maria stood like a statue at the front of the room. If a foot moved or a chair creaked, she flashed a warning smile in that direction.

Maria drew the curtains. She said, "Now listen for a gentle voice to call you by name," and tiptoed from the darkened room. As if the call came with the wind from a far-off hill, the visitors heard a whispered "A-de-li-na!" As quiet as a fawn, Adelina softly left. When she reached the doorway, she laughed and ran to Maria's open arms. As each waited to hear that low, lingering call, not one child moved a muscle. One by one, the children drifted out of the room, their eyes shining, a glow on their faces.

Maria explained that originally she had created the game

of silence to test the children's hearing. To her surprise, she discovered that they enjoyed "making silence."

When the directress played a lively march on the piano, several children got up and marched on the oval line drawn on the floor. Some walked with baskets on their heads, while others carried bells or beanbags on a string that they held perfectly still. Those boys and girls who were intent on what they were doing did not join them. No one said they must. One visitor asked Dominic if the directress always permitted him to do as he liked. He answered, "I do not know if we do as we like, but I know we like what we do."

Lunchtime drew near and the clock struck eleven. That day's four "waiters and waitresses" ate their lunch, then started setting the tables for the others. They kept up a running conversation over the correct placement of the silverware and plates. Moving slowly and carefully, the team produced perfectly set tables. No one said, "Hurry."

When the lunch bell rang, each server very slowly carried a tureen of hot soup to a table and ladled it into the bowls. Maria marveled at how well her waiters and waitresses performed. They stood ready to offer more soup or remove the bowl and bring on the next course. Maria saw spectators moved to tears as they watched four-year-olds serve a meal.

The rest of the day continued in the same easygoing manner. The sleepy ones took naps, while others played outside or worked in the garden.

The number of visitors increased, and the children enjoyed the attention. They brought chairs for the guests, thanked them for coming and for bringing gifts of candy and toys. But the children set these treats to one side. Maria found that the children wanted to do things for themselves

Children at the Casa dei Bambini take turns serving lunch to their classmates.

and did not expect rewards. They cared more for the dressing frames or letter cards. As Elena counted with the number rods, she used a piece of candy merely as a pointer. When a priest brought in a bag of cookies cut in geometric shapes, the children cried out, "See, it's a triangle!" and "I have an oval!" They were more interested in naming the shapes than in eating the cookies.

Educators, newspaper reporters, religious leaders, government officials, and representatives from many countries visited the Casa and gave enthusiastic reports of the happy, well-mannered children. As news of Maria's accomplishments at Casa dei Bambini spread throughout Europe and then throughout the world, teachers begged for more information. And in Rome, other Children's Houses opened

Maria visits her Casa on Via Giusti, set up in a convent in Messina, Italy.

SEVEN

Maria in America

1908–1914

With the opening of each new Montessori school in Rome, Maria always chose an untrained young woman and taught her to run that school. A few of the young women Maria later trained in her teacher-training courses became like daughters to her. They called her *Mammolina,* an Italian name meaning "darling mama," and thought of her as both teacher and mother. Anna Maria Maccheroni, one of Maria's students at the University of Rome's teacher-training college, was the first protégée to join Mammolina's "little family" of close friends and supporters.

In 1907, after hearing Dr. Montessori's inspiring university lecture on what schools should be like, Anna went to the first Casa dei Bambini. She watched Dr. Montessori work calmly and patiently with a three-year-old. She said, "He looked satisfied and happy, just as if he had been given chocolates instead of two new words." After several visits, she knew this was where she wanted to teach. Maria hired her as an assistant. Anna became Maria's friend.

Another Casa dei Bambini opened in Milan in 1908. It was the first to be located outside the city of Rome. Maria placed

Anna Maria Maccheroni in charge. She would have the care of 46 children with one untrained woman to help her. Anna eagerly accepted the job and felt honored that Maria had given her the responsibility.

Queen Margherita was interested in Maria's accomplishments and visited Casa dei Bambini frequently. The queen often invited Maria to the palace to discuss her work. When a terrible earthquake struck the town of Messina in 1908, leaving 60 orphans wandering among the ruins, Queen Margherita helped the nuns in a Franciscan convent set up a Montessori school called Casa on Via Giusti for the children. The depressed orphans had no appetite, couldn't sleep, and cried through the night. Gradually, Maria and the nuns helped them to regain their appetites and sleep peacefully. They became well-mannered, happy "Montessori" children.

In 1908 Maria met Barone and Baronessa Franchetti, who owned a villa near Assisi, not far from Maria's birthplace. The Franchettis were interested in education and used Maria's methods in the primary school they ran for peasant children on their estate. In the summer of 1909, they invited Maria to give the first teacher-training course in her new method at their villa. About one hundred students, mostly teachers from surrounding areas, enrolled in Maria's course. The Franchettis also attended the lectures. Maria taught the students how to run a "Montessori classroom" of two- to six-year-olds and how to introduce her materials to the children in the proper way.

The estate offered a delightful place for Maria to work and rest. She had the hospitality of the Franchettis and the companionship of her enthusiastic assistants, Anna Maccheroni and Anna Fedeli.

Her host urged Maria to write down her teaching

method. "It is your duty," said the Barone. "You might suddenly die and then nothing of it would remain." Maria felt very healthy and had no intention of dying, but she began writing anyway. Within one month, she produced The *Method of Scientific Pedagogy Applied to the Education of Young Children in the Casa dei Bambini,* which described her idea that children learn best through their senses when allowed to teach themselves. This book later appeared as *The Montessori Method.*

DR. MED. MARIA MONTESSORI
DOCENTE ALL'UNIVERSITÀ DI ROMA

IL METODO

DELLA

PEDAGOGIA SCIENTIFICA

APPLICATO

ALL' EDUCAZIONE INFANTILE

NELLE

CASE DEI BAMBINI

CITTÀ DI CASTELLO
TIPOGRAFIA DELLA CASA EDITRICE S. LAPI
—
1909

The title page of the first edition of The Montessori Method

In her book, she wrote, "If we are to develop a scientific system of teaching, we must, then, proceed along lines very different from those which have been followed up to the present time. . . . If a new and scientific pedagogy is to arise from the *study of the individual,* such study must occupy itself with the observation of *free* children."

When she returned to Rome in the fall, Maria found a pile of work. Stacks of letters asked about the method. People from all over the world arrived to see her. She had training courses to plan—she never repeated a lecture because she wanted the material to always be fresh. Students who repeated the course got new material each time. They always heard that a good teacher is one who loves and respects the child. At the close of one training course, Maria said, "We begin with methods of education and culture for the child, and we end by acknowledging that [the child] is our teacher."

In 1910 Edoardo Talamo, the director of the Roman Association for Good Building, expelled Maria from her school at San Lorenzo. He complained that Maria was using the Casa dei Bambini to advertise her method. The public's interest in Montessori had taken away from the importance of his building project. Maria arrived at the San Lorenzo schoolroom to find that Talamo had given the porter orders to prevent her from entering. But rather than being upset, Maria realized she was now free to devote more time to developing her method and training teachers.

A Casa dei Bambini for 45 children opened in Pescheria, a ghetto in Rome, in 1911. Like San Lorenzo, the area was dark, dirty, and disease ridden. The Montessori Method brought changes to all these children's lives. They exploded into writing and reading in the same way the San Lorenzo children had.

Maria reviews copies of her book The Montessori Method.

Maria would have been quite happy to continue treating patients, directing the Children's Houses, and giving lectures. But her dream had become a reality. She felt duty bound to devote all her time and energy to children everywhere. She decided that she must create materials for older children, train teachers, and direct Montessori schools. People who supported her new methods of education were forming Montessori societies and needed her guidance. Her method now became a business and her main source of income. She would no longer lecture at the University of Rome, and she removed her name from the list of practicing doctors. She would now earn her living as a teacher of teachers.

Some of the people who knew Maria and her family never understood the pioneer spirit of this woman. Maria was now the sole supporter of herself, Mario, and her parents, since her elderly father was now retired. Family friends who had once disapproved of her career choice now warned her about giving up her comfortable livelihood as a doctor and a professor. But with her self-confidence and her mother's faith in her, Maria was sure she could support her family. They could live on the proceeds from training courses, her books, and the sale of Montessori classroom materials.

After the long school day, Maria's assistants would gather at the apartment she shared with her parents. Renilde Montessori enjoyed these gatherings. She joined in discussions as the group went over the day's activities. Maria would put on a white apron and prepare an excellent, hearty meal that might include spaghetti, fried potatoes, and veal cutlets. Anna Maccheroni noted that Mammolina did everything with "ease, grace, and exactness of movement."

Maria also liked to relax by doing her own exercises of practical life. She might say, "Quick, quick! Give me my wooden shoes and the water and broom." With great care, she would wash the terrace outside her apartment that overlooked Pincio Park.

Renilde died in December 1912. Besides the loss of her beloved mother, Maria had lost someone who had always been there to advise her, support her decisions, and enjoy her successes. When Renilde died, Maria was like a person turned to stone. She shed no tears and showed no emotion, but she could not eat for three days. Maria turned to work, as she always had during troubled times, but she carried the grief deep in her heart for many years.

After her mother's death, Maria went to visit her son, Mario, as she had many times before. Through the years, Mario had wondered who the "beautiful lady" was who visited him regularly, but he somehow sensed she was his mother. Now a teenager, he asked to go home with her. Maria agreed and from then on, they were together. Still afraid of scandal, Maria introduced him to her acquaintances as her nephew.

By 1911 popular American magazines such as *McClure's Magazine* began carrying articles about Maria Montessori and her method. Samuel S. McClure, owner of the magazine, was a powerful journalist. He invented the Sunday supplement and increased magazine circulation by lowering the subscription rate. He had a "nose for news," and when he heard of the new form of education in Italy, he ordered a journalist to write about it.

Following publication of the articles, a staggering number of inquiries arrived at McClure's office, and Maria was deluged with letters asking how to obtain her book and materials. *McClure's Magazine* did more than any other publication to put Maria's name before the American public. Articles running in the 1911 and 1912 issues were also reprinted in England.

Alexander Graham Bell, the inventor of the telephone,

Inventer Alexander Graham Bell was one of Maria's first American supporters.

was a friend of Sam McClure. Alexander and his wife, Mabel, had several grandchildren and took an interest in their education. They agreed with Maria's criticism of the "butterflies on pins" way of educating. Bell told McClure that he "considered the introduction of the Montessori system in the United States as the most important work that *McClure's Magazine* had ever done." Since the magazine had published many important articles about government, industry, and the armed services, this was quite a compliment to Maria's ideas.

Anne E. George, an elementary schoolteacher, became the first American to travel to Rome and enroll in Maria's eight-month training course. In 1911, Anne started a Montessori school in Tarrytown, New York. She also started a school in the Bells' home in Washington, D.C., the following year.

In response to American teachers' growing interest in the Montessori teaching method, Sam McClure, Anne George, and Mr. and Mrs. Bell formed the Montessori American Committee in 1912. The committee organized the first international training course in Rome. People from all parts of the world attended, including 65 students from the United States.

Students at the first American Montessori school in Tarrytown, New York, learn to use Maria's materials.

As interest in the movement increased, the Montessori American Committee became the Montessori Educational Association with Mabel Bell as president in 1913. Other members included Dorothy Canfield Fisher, the author of books on her visits to Casa dei Bambini; Margaret Wilson, President Woodrow Wilson's daughter; and Sam McClure.

Maria's American supporters thought Dr. Montessori should come to the United States to speak about her ideas in person. In 1913 McClure went to Rome and persuaded her to come to lecture and show films of her schools.

Maria arrived in New York on December 3, 1913, to a royal welcome. Reporters wrote of her as "the most interesting woman in Europe" and "a woman who revolutionized the educational system of the world." They also described her as "motherly looking." In her black dress, dark fur, and large feather-trimmed hat, she looked, as one reporter wrote, "like a galleon under full sail." President Woodrow Wilson sent greetings from the White House. Flags reading "Welcome Doctor Montessori" decorated the streets.

Reporters and photographers crowded into Maria's hotel room. Calmly, she answered their questions in Italian, occasionally slipping into French, as Anne George translated. People milled about. Flashbulbs popped. Maria loved the hubbub. She always enjoyed being the center of attention. Smiling her serene smile, she posed for photo after photo.

One reporter asked Maria why she had come to the United States. She answered, "I came first to America because the work is progressing here rapidly and I want to be sure that it develops in the right way."

When being questioned, she watched the speaker's face closely, perhaps because she wanted the facts taken down in her exact words. Unfortunately, this didn't always happen.

Sam McClure met Maria at the dock when she arrived in New York in 1913.

She made a statement that most toys were too complicated and that parents should not be surprised when a child pulls a toy apart to understand it. The reporter interpreted this statement in a headline that read "Smash Your Toys If You Want To."

Sam McClure had gone to great lengths to publicize a Montessori lecture at New York's huge Carnegie Hall on December 6. Promoters sold five thousand tickets and turned away a crowd of at least a thousand more. Thunderous applause greeted Maria when she stepped onto the stage in a black evening gown. Admirers tossed bouquets to the stage. McClure introduced her as "the greatest woman educator in history." One of her students, Adelia Pyle, translated her two-hour lecture into English.

Maria ended the lecture by saying, "The development at which I aim includes the whole child. My greater aim is the eventual perfection of the human race." She had always emphasized the point that those trained in her method would help to make a better world. Montessori-trained children would grow to be independent, clear thinking, controlled, and responsible.

Alexander Graham Bell invited important officials to a reception for Maria in Washington, D.C. President Wilson canceled a meeting with her when he fell ill, but his daughter Margaret took Maria sightseeing in the White House car. In New Jersey, Thomas Edison took her on a tour of his workshops. Maria lectured in cities from New York to Chicago. Due to public demand, she appeared a second time at Carnegie Hall on December 15.

During her three-week stay, Maria used every spare moment to take notes of ideas to add to her method. She wanted to meet and talk with more Americans, but she had no time. All through the tour, she enjoyed shaking hands. "We never do that in Europe," she said. Though she could not speak the language, she felt she understood American people by the expression in their eyes and the contact of hands.

In April 1914, McClure's brother Robert journeyed to Rome to propose the establishment of an institute in New York that Dr. Montessori would direct. When he arrived, Maria was in her kitchen shelling peas—neatly putting peas in one bowl, pods in another. She said, "I must finish this," and let Robert wait until she was done.

His offer included a library, a lecture hall, and schools for the deaf, the mentally disabled, and normal children. He would provide anything she needed. Maria liked the proposal and for a few days made plans to accept. Then, and with great regret, she decided that to accept the offer meant giving up her freedom. She did not want her work confined to one country. Mario concerned her, too. She could not risk a scandal by moving her son to the United States, and she would not leave him behind in Italy.

When someone suggested that the proposed institute in the United States could mean a fortune for her, Maria shrugged as if that did not matter. She had what was most important in her life—Mario and her mission to teach children to teach themselves.

The San Francisco Panama-Pacific International Exposition attracted people from all over the world to see the latest in art, technology, and education.

···◀ EIGHT ▶···

Going to Catalina

1915

Maria returned to the United States in 1915 when the National Education Association invited her to exhibit her work at San Francisco's Panama-Pacific International Exposition. The 1915 exposition celebrated the completion of the Panama Canal with exhibits of modern technology and innovations from around the world. An exhibit at the exposition would allow Maria to show her teaching method to thousands of people.

Maria planned a model Montessori classroom for her exhibit. Two thousand boys and girls from all social positions and nationalities applied for the 21 places in the class. Maria insisted that those chosen must not have attended school of any kind.

Exposition directors built a room for the Montessori class in the Palace of Education on a raised platform that had a glass wall on one side. Spectators sat in rows of seats beyond the glass.

Dr. Montessori appeared on opening day to teach the class. Spectators saw her bend over a small boy to demonstrate the cylinders. He had to brush the feathers from her enormous hat away from his face.

Helen Parkhurst, a student of Montessori's training course, acted as the directress after the opening day. During the four months of the exposition, people filled the seats every day. At noon, when the children served lunch to their classmates and cleaned up afterward, there was standing room only. The exposition awarded only two gold medals for education. The Montessori class won both.

As always, wherever she traveled, Maria arranged to teach training classes for directresses. The first American course began on May 1, 1915, in Los Angeles. She rented a house there for her "little family" of Anna Fedeli, Adelia Pyle, Helen Parkhurst, and Mario, who was then 16 or 17 years old. He had stayed in Rome with Maria's father during her first visit to America, but she must have felt the time had come for him to take an active part in her life.

Curious neighborhood children wandered into Maria's Los Angeles garden. Whenever she had a group of children around, she could not resist showing them the pink tower and her other materials. The American children took to the Montessori Method's learning "games" as eagerly as their peers across the ocean had.

In spite of success at the exposition, the days in southern California were discouraging for Maria. She wanted her own institute where she could work with children, experiment with educational methods, and train teachers.

When Robert McClure had proposed such an institute, Maria had felt possessive of her method and afraid other people would not present her ideas correctly. In this way, she was her own enemy. Whenever someone suggested building a Montessori institute, she feared she would have to share control and profits, and she rejected the offer.

Maria didn't like her supporters to proceed with a project without first getting her approval. She had a firm rule that a student graduating from her course could teach children, but only Maria herself could train other Montessori teachers. She was annoyed when other authors published books about her method. She claimed they distorted her ideas and the use of her materials. She feared that sales of such books would cut into the profits from her own books.

Maria with students and protégées. Anna Fedeli, Helen Parkhurst, and Adelia Pyle stand at the right in the back row and young Mario stands second from the left in the back.

Although money came in from her books and courses, Maria's debts started to pile up. In Los Angeles, Adelia Pyle hid the bills from Maria. Maria offered Adelia and Helen Parkhurst no pay for their work. Their devotion to her was so strong, they felt Mammolina's grateful thanks and inspiration were payment enough. Without telling Maria, Adelia and Helen wrote to their families for money and told Mammolina not to worry. When their families' money arrived, they paid every bill.

As long as the bills were paid, Maria seemed satisfied and did not question how they were paid. She put on her smile and one of her ridiculous feathery hats and said, "Let's put on perfume and go to Catalina." This phrase became a private joke among the family members. They took the boat to the picturesque island off the California coast, where Adelia and Helen paid for the dinner.

When the classroom exhibit at the exposition closed in November, Margaret Wilson and many other influential people asked Maria to stay in the United States to train teachers. But even the prestige of White House support did not change her mind.

The Montessori Educational Association (MEA) made a conscientious effort to further the Montessori movement in the United States. The members tried to put out a news bulletin, but Maria wanted nothing published about her work without her approval. Some members did not agree when Maria insisted that her preschools teach writing, reading, and arithmetic. She believed children should be free to learn a skill whenever they showed the desire and ability to learn. To her, the possibility of a child writing at the age of four was as certain as the child cutting a new tooth. Without Maria's cooperation, the MEA began to collapse.

Before Maria and the MEA could settle their differences, she received word that her father had died in November 1915. Maria returned to Europe immediately.

So many questions remained unanswered. Who should be in charge? Who should receive money that they raised? How much should Maria get? And most importantly, who would be permitted to train new teachers?

Maria's stubborn streak may have helped her become a doctor, but it hindered her work with American supporters. She insisted on keeping the method "pure" and refused to co-operate with the American societies. She would not accept that even a perfect system could improve when people worked together and shared ideas. In 1916 members of the MEA decided to dissolve the association, and the American Montessori movement ended for a time.

In spite of the success and popularity of her method with many educators, Maria had her critics. One highly respected educator maintained that the method of teaching using the five senses was out-of-date. Instead of the Montessori materials, he said that teachers should give children regular playthings in the classroom. When Maria heard this criticism of her work, she suggested that he open his eyes and see that the things he called impossible were continually happening in her schools.

Clearly, the Montessori movement could not grow in the United States without Maria's supervision. Instead, the movement flourished elsewhere as Maria carried her inspiration and ideas around the world.

As Montessori schools opened around the world, Maria made a point of visiting them and meeting the students.

···◀ NINE ▶···

Maria and Mussolini

1915–1939

By 1915, educational authorities in Spain had heard of the "marvel of San Lorenzo." They invited Maria to establish a Casa dei Bambini in Barcelona. Before leaving for the San Francisco exposition, Maria had sent Anna Maccheroni to Barcelona to open the school. Anna's school started with five children and grew to one hundred pupils in five months. Maria believed that in Barcelona, she had found all the perfect conditions for her institute to train teachers and continue her educational research.

The Barcelona government offered to provide a lovely old Spanish building for an institute. Maria had always hoped for such a paradise setting. There were beautiful gardens, fountains, plenty of room to play, a building for teacher training, and even sheds for animals. She could have classrooms for 3- to 10-year-olds. Maria looked forward to working on new education experiments in these ideal surroundings.

In 1916 Maria gave her first training course at the institute, the Seminari Laboratori de Pedagogia. In spite of the fact that World War I raged across Europe at the time, 185 students enrolled from Spain, Portugal, Great Britain, and the United States. The Spanish government paid part of the course's expenses. The officials of Barcelona arranged for welcoming receptions and entertainment for the students with a holiday atmosphere of national songs and dances.

Maria made one last visit to the United States in December 1917, when she gave a training course in Los Angeles and attended Mario's wedding to Helen Christie, an American.

After the war, Mario and Helen joined Maria in Barcelona to raise their family. Maria would have her grandchildren, Marilena, Mario Jr., Renilde, and Rolando, to watch and enjoy as they grew up. Having these babies with her must have eased the pain of not being able to raise Mario.

Then in 1919, on her 49th birthday, Maria traveled to England to teach a two-month training course. The English welcomed her as the Americans had—like a queen. Again, enthusiastic crowds and receptions greeted her. Newspaper headlines called her arrival "the beginning of a great era for the children of this country." Whenever Maria stepped from a train or a plane, children met her with bouquets of flowers. She acknowledged them with her radiant smile and always seemed to be deeply touched.

Maria's lectures now included methods and materials for 6- to 11-year-olds. In the mornings, teacher trainees learned about the materials and observed children at a Montessori school. Then the trainees listened to Maria's lectures and later practiced teaching as Maria, Anna Maccheroni, and other assistants watched. Each of the trainees took home a copy of Maria's second book, *The Advanced Montessori Method.*

Trainees made an "Apparatus Book" with descriptions of the exercises and drawings of the Montessori materials. After passing written and oral exams, each received a diploma signed by Maria Montessori that stated he or she could teach children, but could not train teachers.

Dottoressa Montessori thanked the class at the end of the course for their excellent work. She suggested that since they had learned the value of silence in working with children, they should part in silence. She seemed visibly moved as all the students silently watched her leave. She turned to give them a last tender look when someone applauded and spoiled the moment. She shook her head, waved her bouquet of white and gold lilies, and hurried off.

Maria was presented to the British court at Buckingham Palace.

When the course ended, Maria set off on a 10-day tour of England. Off and on train after train, she heard welcoming speeches, gave interviews and lectures in crowded halls, and attended receptions. Many cities she visited later organized Montessori societies and opened schools. She returned to England every two years to give a training course.

Everywhere she traveled in Great Britain, Maria visited Montessori schools.

Trouble brewed again. This time members of the London Montessori Society could not agree. Some wanted to follow Maria's method, but others wished to add their own ideas. Maria responded by requesting that her name be withdrawn from the society and resigning as its president.

From London she went to lecture at the University of Amsterdam. Maria called Amsterdam "a town one feels and breathes and in which one loses oneself." In a number of ways, Holland was an ideal country for her teaching method. The government installed her method in the state school system. Because Holland was usually peaceful, political unrest would not likely interrupt her work. Also, a child's liberty was important to parents, who allowed their children to grow up naturally. This attitude toward childrearing fit nicely with Maria's ideas.

Although Barcelona remained the Montessoris' home, strikes and terrorist attacks plagued the city. The Spanish government ceased its support of the institute in 1920 after Maria refused to take any part in their politics.

Maria was almost 50 when she said in an interview, "I don't know what to do." She had made independence a rule of life for herself and for children. But she said that she felt alone "and nobody will ever collaborate. Either they accept what I say, and ask for more, or else they waste precious time in criticizing." Those who called her Mammolina believed in her without question and worshiped her, but she did not consider them her peers. Now she wished that someone would work with her to develop her method. In reality, that seemed impossible, because she would only take a partner who would agree with her completely. She could not accept criticism and did not seem interested in exchanging ideas with a peer.

Maria had not returned to Italy during World War I. Italy had become a poor country, and the government neglected her schools. An Italian group called the Society of Friends of the Montessori Method supported some schools. One beautifully equipped school in a Naples slum had an enrollment of 300 children. Maria's friend, Antonino Anile, became minister of education and arranged for Maria to give a training course in 1922 for teachers at the Naples school.

That year Benito Mussolini took over the government, which became Fascist, a one-party dictatorship. Mussolini came into power aspiring to become a great leader. He would run his country as a well-oiled machine, and the people would bow to his will.

Maria met with Mussolini in 1924 to explain her method. He promised his support, because the idea that children could read and write at an early age appealed to him. Literate citizens would help make a stronger, more productive nation. Also, he could gain acclaim for himself by bringing this world-renowned educator back to Italy. But neither Montessori nor Mussolini seemed to understand each other's policies. Montessori believed in the liberated child. Mussolini believed that liberty was a curse. Nevertheless, Maria was overjoyed that the Italian government would again support Montessori schools.

By 1926 the Montessori movement had spread all across Europe. Austria had many schools in and around Vienna. Ireland had three schools. The Amsterdam Montessori school added classes for children over 12 years old. Italy had Montessori schools in Rome, Milan, Venice, and Maria's home province of Ancona.

From 1923 to 1937, Maria gave courses and saw new Montessori schools and societies established in almost every

*Italian dictator
Benito Mussolini*

country in Europe and South America. Although she had
been in and out of Italy during this time, Mussolini planned a
big celebration in 1930 to honor Dr. Montessori's "return
home." The event also commemorated Rome's first international Montessori training course since 1910. Mussolini saw
to it that all important officials attended the ceremony. He
had Montessori pose beside a large statue of an ancient
Roman. There she stood, middle-aged, short, and heavy in
her close-fitting black hat and old-fashioned long black dress.
To Mussolini, the tableau must have symbolized the glory
of ancient Rome and the famous Dr. Montessori who, at his
direction, had brought culture and education back to Italy.

Maria must have seen Mussolini for what he was—a power-seeking bully. She probably tolerated him as long as she could work without interference. She believed that the Montessori Method could make a difference for Italians. But when she saw small children playing war games with toy machine guns and her former preschoolers wearing Fascist uniforms, she knew there was little hope for her system of education under Mussolini.

Maria strongly objected when Italian children, such as these in the front row, were made to wear military uniforms.

In 1931 Mussolini ordered all teachers to take an oath of loyalty to Fascism. When the Montessori teachers refused to take the oath, he closed all their schools. Maria left Italy and went back to Spain.

During Maria's world travels, Mario was always with her as a devoted son, secretary, business manager, and protector. In 1929 they founded the Association Montessori Internationale (AMI) in Amsterdam with Dr. Montessori as president. The AMI supervised schools throughout the world and kept control of the method and the Montessori materials. Except for Antarctica, every continent had Montessori schools.

The Spanish Civil War began in 1936. General Francisco Franco became dictator of Spain. Friends in England feared for Maria's safety and arranged for the family to leave on a British battleship, with only a few hours' notice. Maria left her possessions, her home, and the educational laboratory of her dreams.

After leaving Spain, Maria needed a new home base. She couldn't return to Rome. In Germany, Adolf Hitler found the Montessori Method contradicted his ideas. He burned her books that mentioned the Catholic religion. A German mob burned Maria in effigy by throwing a stuffed figure representing her into a bonfire.

Ada Pierson, one of her students, was the daughter of a Dutch banker. In 1936 Ada and her parents invited Mammolina, Mario, and his children to stay at their home in Holland after Mario and his wife separated. Remembering Amsterdam from her previous visit, Maria saw the city as a friendly haven. She had once said that the Dutch understood her method of teaching better than any other nation. So when she was not in some other corner of the globe, Amsterdam became her new home.

Peaceful Amsterdam became the permanent headquarters of the Montessori organization in 1929.

Maria and Mario found an ideal spot for an institute in Laren, a village outside Amsterdam. Like Barcelona, Laren offered the perfect setting for her work where no one interfered. They located the institute conveniently near the Association Montessori Internationale, which was still headquartered in Amsterdam.

As in Barcelona, their peaceful existence didn't last. In September 1939, Germany invaded Poland, and Europe entered World War II.

In the meantime, educators had opened many Montessori schools in India and asked for her support. After Mahatma Gandhi visited the Casa dei Bambini in Rome, he and other Indian leaders wanted Maria to establish a teacher-training center in their country. In 1939, when Maria was 69, she and Mario flew the long distance in a small plane to India.

Pictured here with her son, Mario, Maria often wore white flowing robes as she taught and traveled through India.

▸◂ TEN ▸◂

A Peaceful Harbor

1939–1952

Since her days as a medical student, Maria had been lauded and applauded. She had received honor after honor. But the reception in India must have touched her more deeply than any other. The people's outpouring of affection and eagerness to soak up her ideas and put them into practice made her feel she was in a land of promise, close to her heart's desire.

Maria, white-haired and almost 70, kept her usual calm smile and assured manner. One of her Indian students said, "With an air of venerable gracious charm she welcomed each of us as someone precious and dear to her. Though at times we were somewhat awed by her intellect and fine oratory, her captivating smile and shining eyes radiating kind humor endeared her to us all."

Maria would not slow down after the long flight from Holland. With Mario's help, she immediately set about preparing the teacher-training course in the city of Madras.

But India was different in customs, culture, and climate from any other place she had known. Maria, a devout Roman Catholic, noticed that the people of India placed great importance on their own religions in their daily lives. Each home had a corner for prayer or a small shrine. Early in the morning, Maria could hear a *muezzin* call the Muslims to prayer from a tower or minaret.

The camels decorated with bells and flowers fascinated her. Maria rode in a cart pulled by a camel or a rickshaw pulled by a turbaned Indian. "An atmosphere of strange beauty fills these places," she said.

Again, world events intervened. In June 1940, Italy entered World War II against Great Britain. Since India was under British control, the colony's government considered the Italian Montessoris to be enemies of Great Britain. Enemy aliens were ordered to prison camps in all British colonies around the world. The British government finally agreed to let Maria travel about India, but they confined Mario to a prison camp. Maria was dismayed. She had come to depend on him as her translator, her advisor, and her champion.

On Maria's 70th birthday in 1940, the Indians wanted to show their appreciation to her. Maria received a telegram from the viceroy of India, saying, "We thought the best present we could give you was to send you back your son." For the first time, someone had publicly referred to Mario as her son.

The city of Madras built a large hut for the training center. Under a palm leaf roof, from a wicker chair on a platform, Maria faced a sea of three hundred student teachers sitting on mats on the ground. Instead of her usual black dress, she wore a long, flowing white gown with a circle of flowers around her neck.

During the seven years Maria and Mario stayed in India, Maria trained more than a thousand teachers. The students

Maria, who is seated far left, teaches a large group of students in Madras, India. Mario is standing at her side.

sacrificed much to get Montessori training. Many had to travel great distances, others went into debt to pay their way, and some had family objections to overcome.

Maria felt at home in India. The people loved and understood her. After her disappointing experiences with Mussolini in Italy and civil war in Spain, this acceptance felt like being wrapped in a warm comforter. India's leaders praised Maria's work. She met with Rabindranath Tagore, an Indian author who had won the Nobel Prize and established several Montessori schools in India.

Rabindranath Tagore, seen here with some of his students, opened a number of Montessori schools in India.

At the age of 75, Maria wrote to Anna Maccheroni that she was well but losing her energy. Maria said that perhaps "the stimulus of having to struggle is missing."

In 1946 the Montessoris said good-bye to India. The war in Europe was over and Maria needed to resume her teacher-training courses there. They returned to Holland just in time to celebrate Maria's 76th birthday. A month later, they traveled to England for a training course. Former students Phoebe Child and Margaret Homfray met Maria and Mario at the airport to drive them directly to a rented house. But Maria wanted to see London and the results of the bombing during World War II.

After the tour, Miss Homfray wanted to serve tea with a proper tea service, but her silver tea set of mixed and matched pieces embarrassed her. When Maria saw the pitiful tea service, she called for cloths and polish—and without another word, she polished away. That was her style. All things must be clean and shining.

Maria and Mario started a Montessori center in London in 1947 with Homfray and Child as directresses. Soon the two women disagreed with Maria over teacher training. Maria forbade them to issue Montessori diplomas or use her name. Under the direction of Homfray and Child, the school became the St. Nicholas Training Center in London.

As she grew older, Maria continued to travel and teach. Mario was her constant companion.

During Mario's years in India, his children had lived with Ada Pierson's family in Holland. The Piersons also saw that the Montessori work continued in Holland. Mario married Ada in July 1947. Ada and Maria enjoyed each other. Ada often teased her mother-in-law, especially about Maria's frivolous hats.

In August 1947, Maria was nearly 78 years old. From Holland, she and Mario flew to London, and after lunch, boarded a plane for India. Although Maria had already accomplished so much in India, she felt she could do even more. Maria's granddaughter Renilde and Ada joined them in October. For two years, they crisscrossed the country from Madras to Bombay, north to Gwailor, south to Ceylon,

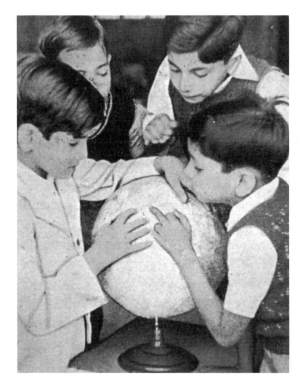

Students study geography in a Montessori school in India.

and north again to Pakistan. They left a trail of schools and training centers throughout India and Pakistan.

In those days, traveling across India was difficult enough for a young person. But Maria had never lost that strength of spirit for doing what she had to do, regardless of the discomforts.

In August 1949, Maria and Mario flew back to Italy for the Eighth International Montessori Congress. Maria spoke before an audience of five hundred members, who were educators from all over the world. They included Catholics, Quakers, Hindus, Muslims, and Buddhists. Despite their different beliefs, she hoped that all could work together for peace throughout the world. She said the fact that they were there to speak and work in cooperation with one another for the same cause reassured her that peace was possible.

Maria had a chance to catch her breath at her home in Amsterdam before going to Paris in December to receive the Cross of the Legion of Honor, France's highest honor.

The United Nations Educational, Scientific and Cultural Organization (UNESCO) invited Maria to speak at the June 1950 conference. This was another great honor. When the announcer introduced her as "someone who has become the symbol of our great expectations for education and world peace," delegates from every nation gave her a standing ovation. Maria received an ovation after every speech she made at the conference.

To a reporter who asked what nationality she was now, Maria replied, "I live in Heaven, my country is a star which turns around the sun and is called the Earth." Actually, many places in Europe called Maria their own. The University of Amsterdam made her a Doctor Honoris Causa, and three Italian cities awarded her citizenship.

When Maria returned from the UNESCO conference, she wrote to her friend Mrs. Joosten in Holland:

> I was greeted with applause when I entered the General Plenary Session of UNESCO. And here in Italy they have conferred upon me a professorship at the University of Perugia. If only I had enough time—to be able to earn them! It is necessary to work hard, isn't it? I met so many interesting people at UNESCO . . . delegates from China, the Philippines, Egypt, Israel, Pakistan—all were friends, all full of enthusiasm. I was surprised to see how alive the idea is among these faraway populations. . . .
> *Viva il bambino!*
> Mammolina

The Ninth International Montessori Congress took place in London in May 1951. In her talk, she discussed not only the preschooler and older child, but also the development of infants. In India, where there were so many babies, she had given much thought to the sensations of infants as they were born. She stressed the bonding of mother and child. She believed that after birth, instead of bundling a baby off to a nursery, a mother should keep her child with her to feed and hold. This has since become common practice.

Maria ended her speech to the congress by saying, "The highest honor and the deepest gratitude you can pay me is to turn your attention from me in the direction in which I am pointing—*the child.*"

"I cannot die; I have too much to do," young Maria had told her mother. Illness could not stop 10-year-old Maria. Now that Maria had turned 80, age could not stop her, either. Up early each day, she worked until all hours of the night. She had never lost her love for food, especially pasta. In spite of being extremely overweight, she insisted she was in good health. She gave a lecture with a toothache, but balked when a dentist said the tooth would have to come out. The year she turned 81, she gave a training course in Austria that lasted from July to October.

On May 6, 1952, Maria sat in a garden in the Dutch village of Noordwijk aan Zee, gazing peacefully across the North Sea and thinking she would like to go to Africa. But her doctors had warned that she was not strong enough to travel. She asked Mario, "Am I no longer any use then?" An hour later, her heart stopped. She was almost 82 years old.

As a "citizen of the world," Maria had always expressed the wish to be buried where she died. Mario followed her wishes and had her buried in a little cemetery of a Roman Catholic church in Noordwijk. The message on her tomb reads, "I beg the dear all-powerful children to unite with me for the building of peace in Man and the World."

A commemorative tablet placed at the Montessori family grave in the cemetery of Rome reads in Italian:

MARIA MONTESSORI
Chiaravalle—August 31, 1870
Noordwijk—May 6, 1952

Famous scientist and pedagogue who dedicated her entire life to the spiritual renewal and to the progress of humanity through the child.

She rests in the Catholic cemetery of Noordwijk [Holland] far away from the country that she had so profoundly loved, far from her loved ones buried there.

This she decided, to give testimony to the universality of her work, which made her a citizen of the world.

Throughout her life, Maria loved to teach children—and be taught by them.

Not until she died could she acknowledge Mario as her son. Her will left everything to *il mio figlio*—"my son."

The stories of Maria's childhood showed traits of self-confidence, leadership, and a desire to help others at an early age. This young girl became the caring, determined, and adventurous woman who would give the world the Montessori Method of Education. Twelve-year-old Maria said that she would never be a teacher—instead Maria Montessori left to the world's children the gift of teaching themselves. She said, "The child's way of doing things has been for us an inexhaustible fountain of revelations."

Maria Montessori left behind a new education. In hundreds of schools throughout the world, children work in open classrooms at child-sized furniture with the pink tower and sandpaper letters, just as children did nearly a century ago at the first Casa dei Bambini.

Sources

p.7   E. M. Standing, *Maria Montessori: Her Life and Work* (New York: New American Library, 1957), 23. Reprinted by permission.

p.9   Norah Smaridge, *The Light Within: The Story of Maria Montessori* (New York: Hawthorn Books, 1965), 18.

p.11   Standing, *Maria Montessori,* 22.

p.13   Ibid., 23.

p.13   Anna Maria Maccheroni, "Maria Montessori," *AMI Communications,* 1966, no. 3, 40.

p.17   Maria Montessori, *The Montessori Method* (New York: Schocken Books, 1964), 14. Reprinted by permission.

p.18   Standing, *Maria Montessori,* 26.

p.18   Rita Kramer, *Maria Montessori: A Biography* (Reading, Massachusetts: Addison-Wesley, 1988), 34.

p.21   Standing, *Maria Montessori,* 24.

p.21   Ibid.

p.21   Ibid., 25.

pp.23–24   Letter to Clara, 1896. Reprinted by permission of Association Montessori Internationale (AMI), Amsterdam, The Netherlands.

p.26   *Maria Montessori: A Centenary Anthology,* edited by AMI (Amsterdam, The Netherlands: AMI, 1970), 5. Reprinted by permission.

p.27   Standing, *Maria Montessori,* 27.

p.29   Letter to Clara, 1896.

p.33   Kramer, *Maria Montessori,* 56.

p.33   *Maria Montessori: A Centenary Anthology,* 14.

p.33   Ibid., 9.

p.36   Anna Maria Maccheroni, *A True Romance: Doctor Maria Montessori As I Knew Her* (Edinburgh, 1946), 4.

p.37   Montessori, *The Montessori Method,* 31.

p.39   Ibid., 38.

p.41   Ibid., 33.

p.45   Standing, *Maria Montessori,* 38.

p.45   Montessori, *The Montessori Method,* 70.

p.46   Ibid., 88.

p.46   Maria Montessori, *The Absorbent Mind* (New York: Dell Publishing Co., 1967), 283.

p.46   Standing, *Maria Montessori,* 38.

p.47   St. Nicholas Training Centre Lectures, Lecture No. 1.

p.53   Standing, *Maria Montessori,* 30.

p.53   Maria Montessori, *The Secret of Childhood* (New York: Ballantine Books, 1981), 129.

p.54   Montessori, *The Montessori Method,* 285.

pp.54–55   Ibid., 287–288.

p.55   Standing, *Maria Montessori,* 47.

p.56   Ibid., 49.

p.56   Montessori, *The Montessori Method,* 270.

p.56   Standing, *Maria Montessori,* 50.

pp.56–57	Montessori, *The Montessori Method,* 300.
pp.58–59	Ibid., 93.
p.60	Montessori, Foreword to *The Secret of Childhood,* xvii.
p.61	Kramer, *Maria Montessori,* 125.
p.63	Maccheroni, *A True Romance,* 7.
p.65	Standing, *Maria Montessori,* 57.
p.65	Montessori, *The Montessori Method,* 28.
p.66	Standing, *Maria Montessori,* 77.
p.68	Anna Maria Maccheroni, "Maria Montessori," *AMI Communications,* 1966, no. 3, 39.
p.70	S. S. McClure, *My Autobiography* (New York: F. Unger Publishers, 1963), 253.
p.72	*New York Tribune,* December 3, 1913.
p.72	"Dr. Montessori Talks of Her Mode of 'Auto-Education,'" *The New York Times,* December 7, 1913.
p.73	*New York Tribune,* December 16, 1913.
p.73	Kramer, *Maria Montessori,* 194.
p.74	Maria Montessori, quoted in *The New York Times,* December 9, 1913.
p.74	Maria Montessori, quoted in *New York Tribune,* December 15, 1913.
p.74	Maccheroni, *A True Romance,* 46.
p.80	Kramer, *Maria Montessori,* 220.
p.84	*London Times Educational Supplement,* September 4, 1919.
p.87	Smaridge, *The Light Within,* 139.
p.87	Sheila Radice, *The New Children: Talks with Maria Montessori* (London: Hodder & Stoughton, 1920), 141–142.
p.95	Smaridge, *The Light Within,* 152–153.
p.96	Ibid.
p.96	*Maria Montessori: A Centenary Anthology,* 47.
p.98	Ibid., 19.
p.101	Ibid., 57.
p.101	Ibid., 50.
p.102	Ibid., 56.
p.102	Standing, *Maria Montessori,* 78.
p.103	Kramer, *Maria Montessori,* 367.
p.103	*Maria Montessori: A Centenary Anthology,* 64.
p.105	Montessori, *The Absorbent Mind,* 179.

Bibliography

Selected Works by Maria Montessori

The Absorbent Mind. New York: Dell Publishing Co., 1967.
The Discovery of the Child. New York: Ballantine Books, 1983.
The Montessori Method. NewYork: Schocken Books, 1964.
The Secret of Childhood. New York: Ballantine Books, 1981.

Other Sources

Association Montessori Internationale (eds.). *Maria Montessori: A Centenary Anthology.* Amsterdam, The Netherlands: Association Montessori Internationale, 1970.
Hainstock, Elizabeth G. *The Essential Montessori.* New York: New American Library, 1978.
Kramer, Rita. *Maria Montessori: A Biography.* Reading, Massachusetts: Addison-Wesley, 1988.
O'Connor, Barbara. *Mammolina: A Story about Maria Montessori.* Minneapolis, Minnesota: Carolrhoda Books, Inc., 1993.
Smaridge, Norah. *The Light Within: The Story of Maria Montessori.* New York: Hawthorn Books, 1965.
Standing, E. M. *Maria Montessori: Her Life and Work.* New York: New American Library, 1957.

Index

Photo Acknowledgments

The photographs have been reproduced with the permission of: Robert Bentley Inc., Cambridge, MA, pp. 1, 44, 47, 48, 49, 50, 55, 62, 71; UPI/Bettmann, pp. 2, 73; Association Montessori Internationale, Amsterdam, pp. 6, 9, 14, 20, 28, 40, 67, 79, 82, 85, 86, 94, 97, 99; Moro Roma, Archivio Fotographico with the assistance of Dr. Pietro de Santis and Dr. Maria Luisa Tabasso of Centro Nazionale Montessori, Roma, and the Garzanti family, Milan, pp. 10, 12, 17, 34, 37, 51, 52, 58, 61, 65, 90, 100, 104; Boston Medical Library in the Francis A. Countway Library of Medicine, p. 25; The Bettmann Archive, pp. 30, 76; Library of Congress, pp. 70, 89, 92; Archive Photos, p. 98

Front cover photograph: Association Montessori Internationale, Amsterdam. Back cover photograph: Archive Photo/Popper Foto.